NEW ZEALAND

AOTEAROA

NEW ZEALAND
AOTEAROA

CRAIG POTTON

CONTENTS

Pages 2-3: Abel Tasman National Park; *pages 4-5*: Mt Tasman,
Aoraki/Mount Cook National Park; *left*: Mackay Falls, Milford
Track, Fiordland National Park

NORTH ISLAND

CAPE REINGA

NINETY MILE
BEACH

Bay of Islands

Kerikeri •
Waitangi • • Russell

*Hokianga
Harbour*

• Whangarei

Pacific Ocean

*Hauraki
Gulf*

• Coromandel
• Whitianga

Auckland •
Piha •
*Manukau
Harbour*

Thames • • Whangamata

Waihi •

WHITE
ISLAND

Mt Maunganui ▲
Tauranga •

Bay of Plenty

Tasman Sea

Hamilton •

EAST
CAPE

Waitomo Caves •

Rotorua •

• Tolaga Bay

*Lake
Taupo* • Taupo

*Lake
Waikaremoana*

• Gisborne
Poverty Bay

New Plymouth •

▲ MT TONGARIRO
▲ MT NGAURUHOE
▲ MT RUAPEHU

▲ MT TARANAKI

Hawke Bay

• Napier
Havelock North •

CAPE
KIDNAPPERS

Wanganui •

Palmerston North •

KAPITI ISLAND

Masterton •

• Castlepoint

Wellington •

• Martinborough

Cook Strait

8

SOUTH ISLAND

FAREWELL SPIT

Golden Bay

Collingwood

Takaka

Marlborough Sounds

Tasman Bay

Karamea

Nelson

Picton

Blenheim

Westport

St Arnaud

Punakaiki

Tasman Sea

Greymouth

Kaikoura

Hokitika

Arthur's Pass

Franz Josef

MT TASMAN

Christchurch

Fox Glacier

AORAKI/MT COOK

Bruce Bay

BANKS PENINSULA

Lake Tekapo

Lake Pukaki

Tekapo

Fairlie

MT ASPIRING

Timaru

Lake Wanaka

Milford Sound

Wanaka

Queenstown

Arrowtown

Oamaru

Lake Wakatipu

Moeraki

Lake Te Anau

Pacific Ocean

Te Anau

Lake Manapouri

Dunedin

Invercargill

Foveaux Strait

Mason Bay

STEWART ISLAND

WEST COAST

Spanning 600 km from Karamea in the north to the Cascade River in the south, the West Coast region is uncompromising in its abundant mountainous beauty, as well as in its climate. The area's eastern border is dominated by the Southern Alps, an unbroken line of mountains, from which glacier tongues creep towards rainforests, and rivers make swift passage towards the Tasman Sea. Waterfalls, lakes, wildlife and a wild coastline complete the catalogue of natural icons, which are often startling when encountered. Nowhere else in New Zealand is nature's work so evident.

The 'West Coasters' who occupy the margins of this essentially primeval landscape are easily the most stoic and individualistic of any New Zealand community; on many occasions they have pitted themselves against outside influences in order to preserve lifestyles firmly rooted in their pioneering past.

Although forests on river and coastal plains have been felled for settlement, farming and timber, the West Coast, nevertheless, remains the least modified area of developed New Zealand. The significance of Westland's landscapes lies not only in their scenic value but also in their importance as ecological sanctuaries. The region's vast podocarp and beech forests and accompanying wildlife are outstanding living representations of primeval life-forms that existed millions of years ago. As well as providing havens for many endangered or rare species, the West Coast wetlands, and the large areas of kahikatea and rimu forests in particular, are the last of any great size of their kind in New Zealand. In 1989 the United Nations bestowed 'World Heritage' status on the mountain and forest lands of South-West New Zealand because of their exceptional value as one of the world's great wilderness regions.

Extractive industries – timber, gold, coal and greenstone – and in the last 20 years, the conservation movement, form a huge part of the region's history. For centuries Maori traders traversed the Southern Alps (no easy accomplishment even by modern standards) or came by sea to deal in greenstone won from West Coast rivers. Although the series of gold rushes that began in 1864 saw the local population swell from a few hundred to 30,000 in the space of a year, it was coal mined from seams in the southern Paparoas and on the Buller Plateau north of Westport that would prove the region's most enduring revenue earner. Coal towns like Blackball, Granity and Denniston, ports at Greymouth and Westport and the transalpine railway across Arthur's Pass were founded and survive on the strength of 'black gold' reserves.

The destruction of West Coast forests inevitably led to clashes between 'greenies' and developers. In the 1970s and 1980s some of the hardest fought conservation battles in New Zealand were acted out over proposals to log North and South Westland lowland forests. The establishment of Paparoa National Park, additions to Westland National Park and the preservation of South Westland forests came about after some lengthy and bruising campaigns. Recently, entrepreneurial West Coasters have turned the region's economic focus away from resource depletion to one in which the appreciation of the region's primeval splendour is paramount. Significantly, tourism now outstrips all of the extractive industries as a revenue earner.

Rain on the West Coast, sometimes lasting for days or months on end, is something of a legend; annual rainfall statistics range from 2000 mm at Westport, 5000 mm at Franz Josef and upwards of 10,000 mm in the high mountains and valleys. But the West Coast can pour on sunshine as well, particularly in late summer and mid-winter. The vigorous climate has not put off those drawn by the lifestyle offered. Craftspeople, artists, writers, adventurers, nature lovers and seekers of solitude take their place alongside miners, farmers and hardened old-timers. When citizens get together, it's usually accomplished in the incomparable style of events like the annual Hokitika Wild Food Festival, where it is possible to feast on such delicacies as possum pate, chamois kebabs, goat curry and the ever-traditional feed of whitebait patties.

Left: South Westland's Lake Matheson moments before a winter sunrise.

At Punakaiki in North Westland the wind, rain and sea have eroded spectacular canyons and blowholes from the limestone/mudstone edge. These are the renowned pancake rocks of Paparoa National Park. The blowholes are easily viewed from a walking track, and are most active when a southwesterly swell is running.

Westland National Park's Franz Josef Glacier, Ka Roimata o Hine Hukatere, is one of the fastest moving glaciers in the world – averaging 2–3 metres a day. Since 1865, the glacier's terminal has retreated more than 3 km and will continue to retreat despite the occasional surge after a heavy winter. *Right*: A classic vista across Westland National Park toward the Southern Alps, from the coast at Waikukupa. *Overleaf*: Lush South Westland rainforest.

Evening views in South Westland: *Above*: The vista across Bruce Bay and the forests of the Te Wahipounamu World Heritage Area to the summits of Aoraki/Mt Cook and Mt Tasman. *Left*: A lagoon at mouth of the Cook River, south of Fox Glacier. *Far left*: Ohinemaka Beach, a wonderful sweep of coastline flanked by ancient dunes and wetlands.

The icy summits of Tasman (left) and Aoraki/Mt Cook rise dramatically above farmland near Fox Glacier village. At the base of the foothills is the boundary of two of the earth's continental plates – the Indo-Australasian and the Pacific. This fault – the Alpine Fault – is responsible for lifting the Southern Alps to its present height. The fault comes ashore at Milford Sound and can be traced all the way to Marlborough.

Top: A remote homestead at Inangahua, in North Westland. Further north, on the coastal strip near Karamea, a grove of nikau palms is lit by evening light (*above*).

Above: A guide takes a tour party through a Fox Glacier ice cave. Guided walks on the lower parts of the glacier offer a spectacular introduction to this icy environment. *Right*: Towering seracs on the glacier's terminal face. *Far right*: A dramatic aerial view of the Fox Glacier as it plunges to the lowlands from its tributary snowfields below Mt Tasman. *Overleaf*: Sunset, Lake Matheson, Fox Glacier.

Left: Sunset on a remote West Coast beach near Karamea, in North Westland. *Above*: A walker dwarfed by the enormous overhang on the Truman Track, a popular coastal track near Punakaiki in Paparoa National Park.

Winter on the névés, ridges and summits of Westland National Park, in these aerial views taken at dusk. The broad névé in the image above is the snowfield feeding the Franz Josef Glacier, while the prominent peak above the névé is Elie de Beaumont. *Right*: Three-thousand metre peaks above Fox Glacier, from left, Mt Haast, Lendenfeld Peak, Mt Tasman and Torres Peak – each presenting considerable challenges to mountaineers.

Morning mist lifts on a frosty morning at Lake Mapourika (*left*) north of Franz Josef. Lake Mapourika is one of a string of beautiful forest-fringed lakes that were formed when glaciers retreated at the end of the last Ice Age. These lakes are important habitat for native fish such as eels and galaxids, and waterfowl. Many of them have been stocked with trout, offering West Coast anglers (*above*) both a challenge and a feed. *Previous pages*: Little Arch, Oparara Valley, Kahurangi National Park.

Beech forest (*above*) flanking the Oparara River in Kahurangi National Park. South of Kahurangi, in Paparoa National Park, tall tree ferns and juvenile nikau palms dominate the coastal forest pictured at far left. This park contains a significant lowland forest of mixed beech and podocarp forest which is seen here (*left*) spreading from the coast to the base of the Paparoa Range up the Fox River.

Lake Gault, lying atop a glacial moraine against the backdrop of the Southern Alps, fills a hollow left as the Franz Josef Glacier retreated more than 10,000 years ago. Glaciers are estimated to have extended 20 km beyond the present coastline at the height of the last Ice Age, a time of far lower sea levels. *Top right*: The terminal face of the Franz Josef dwarfs walkers on a guided walk on the glacier. Kea (*lower right*), an audacious mountain parrot, are a relatively common sight in New Zealand mountain areas.

CANTERBURY

Over millions of years, wind, water and ice age glaciers have smoothed the Canterbury landscape, in the process creating the largest expanse of flat land in New Zealand. The Canterbury Plains, today a virtually treeless chequerboard of ordered rural fields, are almost 200 km long and 70 km at their widest. In the west, the plains end abruptly against a line of steeply rising Southern Alps' foothills. This line is broken by a series of immense rolling highcountry tussock basins (the largest being the Mackenzie Basin) in the upper catchments of the region's major river systems. Swiftly flowing braided waterways – including the Rakaia, Rangitata, Waimakariri and the Waitaki – follow paths scoured by ancient glaciers to the plains below where they continue spreading massive amounts of eroded leavings from the Alps.

The backdrop to the area, the Alps, reach their zenith in South Canterbury in Aoraki/Mount Cook National Park, the country's most important assemblage of mountains. It is these mountains whose retreating glaciers have left behind the northern 'great lakes' – Tekapo, Pukaki and Ohau. Substantial peaks, valleys and glaciers stretch as far north as Arthur's Pass National Park. In many places native beech forest intervenes between tussocklands and mountains.

Canterbury's other prominent landscape feature projects into the Pacific Ocean. Banks Peninsula owes its existence to two volcanoes that ceased erupting about five million years ago. Once an island, the peninsula was eventually linked to the mainland by alluvial outpourings from the Alps. Over time, the sea has breached the extinct craters of the two volcanoes to form Lyttelton and Akaroa harbours.

The absence of forests in Canterbury dates to early Polynesian settlers who dwelt in large numbers by the coast and on the plains during the 'moa hunter' era. Naturally occurring fires, and those lit to flush the now extinct flightless moa from the forests, were uncompromising in their destruction of vegetation and wildlife. Thus, it was that a huge plain of golden tussocklands greeted the first European, filling them with well-justified hopes for agriculture. The founders of 'European' Canterbury entertained grand visions of vast grazing runs owned by gentlemen farmers, although in practice the plains were more suited to small holdings of mixed cropping and livestock. In fact, it was in the foothills and highcountry tussocklands where large sheep runs were created and the gentlemen farmers found the riches they hoped for.

Modern Canterbury is the most populous area in the South Island, with most of its 500,000 inhabitants found in the sprawling environs of Christchurch. The local economy is still based on the wool, meat and crop production of the plains and hill farms around which have grown numerous robust towns and villages. Christchurch is the region's major commercial centre, with an international airport, university and numerous cultural institutions. Central city parks, oak-lined avenues, the meandering Avon and Heathcote rivers, gothic and Victorian architecture, wealthy private schools, the Anglican cathedral, and even its smog, endow the city with its slightly contrived English character.

Mixed blessings have accrued from the region's climate which is regularly demonstrated by its extremes. Nothing is quite as pervasive as Canterbury's famous nor'wester, a hot, dry and dusty wind, which is usually heralded by dramatic cumulus arches over the mountains. This fohn wind sweeps across the plains raising temperatures and testing tempers of town and country folk alike. Nor'westers are often followed by chilling southerlies that dump snow on the hills and plains, causing havoc for sheep farmers, and anticipation in the minds of winter sports enthusiasts.

Travellers have long enjoyed a Christchurch stopover on the tourist trail to the mountains, Queenstown and beyond. New Zealanders too, appreciate the region's offerings, ranging from winter skiing, salmon fishing or journeys into the mountains of Arthur's Pass – all within two hours of Christchurch.

Left: The Devil's Punchbowl, a short walk from Arthur's Pass village in Arthur's Pass National Park. *Overleaf*: The ice ramparts of Aoraki/Mt Cook, New Zealand's highest peak, in Aoraki/Mount Cook National Park.

Cathedral Square, Christchurch: the Gothic architecture of the 19th century Christchurch Cathedral contrasts with the work of 21st century sculptor Neil Dawson, whose 18 m Chalice was erected to celebrate the new millennium and the 150th Anniversary of the founding of Christchurch. The cathedral is one of several notable Canterbury landmarks designed by architect Benjamin Mountfort. A tram route links Cathedral Square with Christchurch's latest architectural statement, the new Christchurch Art Gallery, which opened in 2003. The Canterbury rugby team (in red and black), habitual winners of the national provincial championship, are seen here in action in Christchurch's Jade Stadium.

Canterbury's generous plains reach in every direction west towards distant ranges and mountains. Basil Dowling, writing in the 1940s, perceived the plains bleakly – 'a vast emptiness' where 'tree is miles from tree/Except where in dark ranks they muster/Against the gales or cluster/Befriending lonely farms'. At 64 km wide, and almost 200 km long, the plains are the largest expanse of flat land in New Zealand. (Photograph: Andris Apse)

Top: Some people see cute and cuddly in the spring-time – others see lamb chops. Meanwhile, at Castle Hill (on SH 73 between Christchurch and Arthur's Pass) cattle graze farmland beneath limestone outcrops at Castle Hill Reserve, a popular rock climbing and walking locale.

Above: The tussock-covered foothills on the eastern side of the Southern Alps are home to a string of vast high country sheep stations. Here on a South Canterbury station a shepherd musters a flock of merino sheep, a breed favoured in this harsh country for their hardiness and for the lucrative ultra-fine wool they produce. (Photograph: Andris Apse) On easier terrain (*right*) a farmer on the ubiquitous four-wheeler drives his stock down a country road with the help of his dogs.

Canterbury's nor'wester, a fohn wind that rushes off the Main Divide, is often heralded by spectacular cloud formations such as these over Lake Tekapo (*above*) and in North Canterbury (*left*). Lindis Pass Scenic Reserve (*far left*), a beautiful region of tussock grasslands, lies on the Canterbury/Otago border. *Overleaf:* Fairlie pastureland under a thick blanket of snow.

Aoraki/Mount Cook National Park is New Zealand's premier alpine park. From the summit of Aoraki/Mt Cook (*above*) come views south toward Lake Pukaki and the Mackenzie Basin. *Far left*: The south face of Aoraki/Mt Cook from the Hooker Valley, near the Hermitage. *Left*: An aerial view of the eastern side of the Malte Brun Range, above the cloud-covered Murchison Glacier.

DEEP SOUTH

Celebrated for its lake and mountain scenery, the landscapes of the Deep South form some of the country's most distinctive landscapes. In the west rise the mountains of Fiordland and Mount Aspiring national parks – two large and uncompromising wilderness regions – the former presenting a daunting topography carved from erosion-resistant granites, diorite and gneiss, the latter a less steep land formed from more brittle schists. East of the parks lie settled lands: the starkly beautiful tussock plateaux and valleys of Central Otago, studded with schist outcrops and cut through with spectacular gorges. Ice, wind and rain have continued to work these landscapes, but the most important influence on the shape of mountain, basin and range was the repeated advance and retreat of glaciers and ice sheets during the past two million years, which left in their wake the 'great' southern lakes: Te Anau, Manapouri, Wanaka, Hawea and Wakatipu. These lakes, and the national parks are now part of the Te Wahipounamu South-West New Zealand World Heritage Area.

In Maori mythology the South Island's glacial lakes were created by Rakaihautu, a revered chief who excavated huge furrows that filled with water. The first peoples, prevented by the southern climate from establishing gardens (and thus permanent settlements), were hunter-gatherers who discovered abundant birdlife, including the giant flightless moa, which here as elsewhere was hunted to extinction. As the more sophisticated Maori society arose, the trade in pounamu, a jade found on the shores of Lake Wakatipu, in the Dart Valley and Milford Sound assumed great economic significance. Pounamu was traded throughout the country but intertribal warfare over the control of this and other resources lasted several centuries before Europeans arrived.

The Maori population, already reduced by intertribal wars over greenstone, was confined to small coastal settlements. The Maori community was further reduced by an outbreak of measles, brought by the Europeans, and against which the Maori had no immunity.

Within decades of Captain Cook sighting and mapping New Zealand's shores, bands of transitory European sealers were busy in the south where they plundered (and almost exterminated) fur seals from all around the southern coastline. In 1806 one shipment alone carried more than 60,000 skins to Sydney furriers. Resolute and hardworking Scots settlers eventually stamped a long-term mark on the south. They sailed into Otago harbour in 1848 and set out to establish major sheep runs in the tussocklands of Otago and Southland. Well used to harsh climates and terrain, the Scots built robust towns like Oamaru and Balclutha and the cities of Invercargill and Dunedin. In May 1861, a Tasmanian prospector struck gold in Central Otago, sparking a gold rush that transformed Otago. Gold towns like St Bathans, Arrowtown and Queenstown were founded. Some of these towns still survive today, while others are merely ghostly remnants, now tourist attractions in themselves. For a time, Dunedin became New Zealand's richest city. Examples of Victorian architecture – among them the university, Larnach Castle and Dunedin Railway Station – remain among the country's finest illustrations of the age.

Faced with economic decline in the latter half of this century, the citizens of Otago and Southland have had to work hard to reverse the northward drift of industry and people. Fishing and sheep farming underpin the economy and large industrial developments such as the Bluff aluminium smelter continue to provide jobs. In Central Otago, tourism, centred around Queenstown and Wanaka, has expanded rapidly beyond the traditional attractions of mountains, lakes, famous walks and skiing to encompass a range of adventure activities, historical tours and 'eco' tours. New areas have also opened up. More people are now visiting the Catlins coast in the region's southeast corner and across Foveaux Strait, Stewart Island is increasingly popular with trampers, sea-kayakers and nature lovers seeking adventure on the edge of the vast Southern Ocean. Stewart Island now boasts New Zealand's latest national park – Rakiura – gazetted in 2002.

Left: Sunset on Tititea/Mt Aspiring, in Mount Aspiring National Park. *Overleaf*: A sparkling winter's morning at Milford Sound after a southerly clearance, in Fiordland National Park.

Three images of the Milford Track: an alpine tarn on Mackinnon Pass (*above*), the highpoint of the track, surrounded by alpine grasses and shrubs. Mt Elliot is the peak behind; beech forest (*left*) in the Clinton Valley on the approach to Mackinnon Pass; (*far left*) Sutherland Falls, fifth highest waterfall in the world, drains Lake Quill and plunges into the Arthur Valley, the route to Milford Sound.

Top: A tramper in the Routeburn valley completes the three-day Routeburn Track walk. *Above*: Fiordland was the last place on the mainland where native kakapo, a flightless parrot, were found. Under severe threat of extinction from introduced predators, the last kakapo were removed and placed on offshore islands. Fewer than 100 birds remain today. *Left*: Red and silver beech forest in Fiordland's Eglinton valley. *Overleaf*: Lake Hawea.

A winter vista on the St Bathans Downs, one of the scenes of the 1860s Otago gold rush. Thousands of diggers swarmed to the area, and numerous settlements rose from the landscape. Ghost towns such as Bendigo (*right*) are all that remain of many of these places, the exception being St Bathans where several rush-era wooden and stone buildings provide a focal point for the Otago Goldfields Park.

Far left: According to Maori lore, the 60 million-year-old Moeraki Boulders (halfway between Oamaru and Dunedin) are petrified food baskets from a great waka (canoe) that foundered near here. *Above*: High above Dunedin's Otago Harbour, a single ti kouka (cabbage tree) is battered by a northerly sweeping across Otago Peninsula. Among the peninsula's natural attractions are breeding colonies of the yellow-eyed penguin (*left*).

The clear pools of the Clinton River at Clinton Forks (*above*) on the southern leg of Fiordland's Milford Track. Once described as the finest walk in the world, the Milford Track joins Lake Te Anau with Milford Sound. *Right*: Morning mist clears from Campbells Kingdom, an area near Doubtful Sound in Fiordland National Park. *Previous pages*: The Townley and Wall ranges of Fiordland National Park, west of Lake Manapouri.

Although the 1860's goldrush contributed much toward Central Otago's character and history, it was gold in the form of wool that was the real source of the region's prosperity, resulting in the conversion of tussock landscapes (*left*) for sheep and wool farming. Founded during the gold rush, Arrowtown, with nearby Lake Hayes (*top*) and its historic miners' cottages (*above*), is now a popular tourist and holiday destination.

Queenstown, picturesquely sited on the shores of
Lake Wakatipu beneath The Remarkables, is
often dubbed the country's adventure capital. Bungy
jumping, jetboating, rafting, skiing, paragliding,
mountainbiking and mountaineering are among the
adventurous activities to be enjoyed here.

The half-day walk from the Milford Road to Key Summit (*far left*) is rewarded with fine views from a forest-fringed alpine wetland toward Mt Christina in Fiordland's Darran Mountains. Lake Te Anau (*above*) is one of the area's large and beautiful glacier-formed lakes. Fiordland's blocky granite peaks contrast with the more erodable greywacke/schist ranges (*left*) seen near Wanaka to the northeast.

The Southern Ocean pounds Fiordland's wild south coast (*left*) creating features such as this impressive arch. Across Foveaux Strait is Stewart Island, the bulk of which is now contained within Rakiura National Park. Tramping and hunting are popular recreational activities – (*top*) a tramper is seen here at West Ruggedy beach on Rakiura's northwest circuit, which includes Mason Bay's dunelands (*above*).

Top: Mt Tutoko (left) and Mt Madeline are Fiord-
land National Park's highest peaks in one of the most
challenging alpine climbing areas in New Zealand.
Above: Chalky Island, on the South Fiordland coast.
Right: Stunning glaciated peaks above Milford
Sound.

81

NELSON MARLBOROUGH

Nelson and Marlborough have few peers when one considers the attractive lifestyles, the pleasant climate and the wide spectrum of coastal and alpine landscapes that they offer. Together, the two regions occupy the whole of the northern South Island, a landscape that is overtly mountainous but which also features fertile plains on which their 120,000 inhabitants live. People relish a slower-paced life in close proximity to bush-fringed mountains and superb coastal areas.

Nelson and Marlborough are easily the most diverse areas in New Zealand in terms of their geology, climate and native plants and animals. Some of the the country's oldest rocks (450 million-year-old granite and gneiss) are found in the wetter forest-clad ranges of Kahurangi National Park, while some of the youngest rocks (25 million years) are found in the arid, less vegetated Inland and Seaward Kaikoura ranges of southeastern Marlborough. The mountains of Nelson Lakes National Park mark the northern extent of the Southern Alps while the Kaikoura mountains feature the region's highest peak, the 2885 m Mt Tapuae-o-Uenuku.

The presence of significant strongholds of native plants and animals within these landscapes is due largely to this wide range of habitats and climatic zones, and the lesser effects of the ice ages on the northern South Island. A remarkable 65 percent of New Zealand's 2200 species of surviving native plants are found here and of these, 130 are endemic to the region. Unique animals such as the tuatara – a living link with the dinosaurs, the Nelson cave spider, Hamilton's frog and the Stephens Island gecko all find refuge here.

The 2500 km coastline is one of the longest of any region. Here rugged boulder beaches on the Kaikoura coast contrast with the low-lying windswept sand dunes of Farewell Spit on Golden Bay's western shores. Between Tasman Bay and Golden Bay lies the exceedingly popular Abel Tasman National Park coast, where native forests touch the shores and perfect crescent beaches alternate with blocky granite headlands. East of Tasman Bay are the Marlborough Sounds, a weaving 1400 km coastline of islands and drowned river valleys that have become a playground for holidaymakers, yachties, anglers and divers. Interspersed along the entire Nelson-Marlborough coast are several significant coastal wetlands and lagoons, including the internationally recognised Farewell Spit, a feeding and breeding ground for an enormous number of migratory and endemic birds.

No less than 40 percent of Nelson and Marlborough is under some form of conservation protection in recognition of the ecological, wilderness and recreational values that are present. Nelson Lakes, Abel Tasman and Kahurangi national parks, and Mt Richmond Forest Park are the largest of these protected areas, offering unsurpassed wilderness adventures for the experienced and self-reliant.

Human settlement in Nelson and Marlborough began with the Maori who established permanent villages and seasonal camps throughout the two regions, particularly in food-rich coastal areas like the Marlborough Sounds. Although Maori are fewer in number today, many tribes maintain sacred and practical affiliations with the landscape. European sealers, whalers and, eventually, settlers followed the explorers Abel Tasman and James Cook, and new settlements sprang up in all the region's major river valleys. Nelson was established in 1842, on the edge of a natural harbour and today is one of the more enduring and pleasant provincial cities. Port Nelson harbours the country's largest fishing fleet while the surrounding rural environment supports a thriving fruit-growing industry and the second largest exotic forest plantation in the country. Across the dividing Richmond ranges, Marlborough's economy, founded on dairy and sheep farming, has been boosted by a burgeoning wine industry, marine farming and horticulture. Tourism has grown rapidly in both regions, proving a boon for smaller centres such as Picton, Havelock, Kaikoura, Motueka and Takaka. And while there is a strong emphasis on 'eco-tourism' focusing on the region's parks and waterways, festivals celebrating wine, food and the arts are now major drawcards. There is nothing more spectacular than Nelson's wearable art awards, which has drawn national and international acclaim. The 'World of Wearable Art', a permanent collection of memorabilia from past shows is now one of Nelson city's top tourist attractions.

Left: Awaroa Inlet, Abel Tasman National Park.

Abel Tasman National Park's sublime forest-fringed
bays and golden-sand beaches are connected by the
most popular tramping route in New Zealand – the
Coast Track. At Pukatea Bay (*above*), a tramper takes
a break to stroll along the edge of this perfect crescent
beach. At high summer, the park's beaches are packed
with people who have arrived on foot, or by yacht,
boat or kayak. *Right*: Torrent Bay. *Previous pages*:
Windshorn coastal forest at Puponga Farm Park,
Golden Bay.

Sea kayaking is a popular Abel Tasman coast experience, providing opportunities to encounter seals, dolphins, penguins and other coastal wildlife. Kayakers also see the park's impressive granite headlands and unusual formations such as Split Apple Rock (*above*). *Top:* Tree ferns line a streamway near the coast.

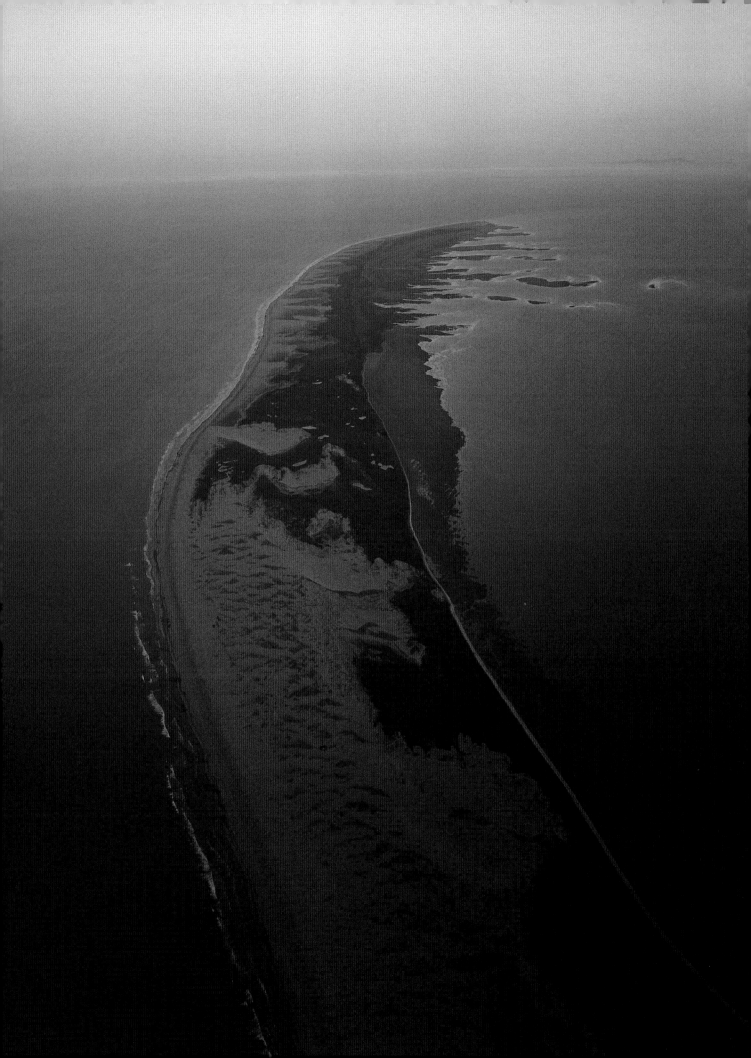

Farewell Spit (*far left*), a sheltering arm across Golden Bay, arcs eastward in this sunset image. The spit's shallow inner coast is an internationally recognised and protected wetland used by the tens of thousands of migratory birds that gather here between September and March. Golden Bay's main industry, other than tourism, is dairy farming, which takes place on the coastal lowlands and river valleys backing onto Kahurangi National Park.

Nelson Haven, the Boulder Bank and Tasman Bay, from Nelson's Port Hills (*left*), looking towards the Abel Tasman Coast. Nelson City (population 41,500) is a thriving regional centre, a hub for the tourism, horticulture, forestry and fishing industries, and increasingly a place for wealthy retirees. *Top*: Blue Lake, Nelson Lakes National Park. *Above*: Cricket is one of New Zealand's popular summer sporting pastimes. Here, a club match is played on a sunny Nelson afternoon.

The sheltered bays and coves of the Marlborough
Sounds, ancient valleys drowned by rising seas, are a
modern-day yachting paradise. Yachts are seen here
moored near Lochmara Bay, in Queen Charlotte
Sound (*above*). In this aerial view (*right*) are the
forested ridges of Mt Richmond Forest Park, Pelorus
Sound, Admiralty Bay and D'Urville Island on the
edge of Cook Strait.

Traditional industries such as sheep farming (*far left*) and crop-growing are the mainstay of the Marlborough economy, but the region's climate and soils have also proved ideal for grapes. Vast areas of the Wairau valley (*above*) have been converted to vineyards – Marlborough is now the country's largest wine region, and is world famous for the quality of its sauvignon blanc. *Left*: Sunrise on the Kaikoura coast, south of Blenheim, looking towards the Seaward Kaikoura Range.

98

Once hunted to near extinction, sperm whales (*left*) are now the focus of a major whale-watching industry at Kaikoura, south of Blenheim. New Zealand fur seals, which breed along the coast, and dolphins (*top*: common dolphin at left, dusky dolphin at right) are common sights, much to the delight of visitors.

AUCKLAND &
THE FAR NORTH

Northern New Zealand tapers gently to a sandy duneland peninsula where the Tasman Sea and Pacific Ocean roar in unison as they converge off Cape Reinga. Only 10,000 years ago seas surrounding the region were locked in ice. The eastern coastline stretched as far as Great Barrier Island, and the Coromandel Peninsula was joined to the main northern land mass. As the ice ages ended, oceans rose to engulf low-lying land, creating bays and gulfs, making islands of volcanoes and high hills, and fashioning harbours from ancient river valleys.

Between Auckland's Manukau harbour and Cape Maria van Diemen, the Far North's west coast presents a long and straight edge of beach and duneland. The east coast is more complex, a ragged edge with numerous bays, inlets and estuaries. Both coasts have been breached by natural harbours but the west's Hokianga, Kaipara and Manukau harbours impress in the size and intricacy of their waterways that penetrate far into the interior.

Millions of years of volcanic activity in the north has left a distinctive legacy of cones and lava flows, overlaying an even older sedimentary landscape. The metropolis of Auckland is constructed on a volcanic field from which more than 60 volcanoes have erupted. None are active today but the nonchalant might remember that Rangitoto Island, the classically proportioned cone opposite the entrance to Waitemata harbour, erupted just 600 years ago.

Humid summers and wet winters are marks of a subtropical climate – indeed these northern parts enjoy the warmest weather (although not necessarily the sunniest) of all the country. The mangrove-lined estuaries and harbours found throughout the north (and nowhere else) are further evidence of tropical influences. The agreeable climate and once abundant natural resources of fish, shellfish and forests lured early Polynesian settlers, who also found excellent growing conditions for the kumara, yams and taro they brought from their Pacific homelands. The north became one of the most densely settled areas of New Zealand and imprints of Maori habitation are found on most headlands, bays and islands, as well as on the volcanic cones of the Auckland area.

Following patterns typical of European colonisation anywhere in New Zealand, migratory whales, gold and forests around the region were heavily exploited. Discovery of the unsurpassed qualities of kauri for boat building rang the death knell for Northland's enormous kauri forests. Kauri timber and its gum were New Zealand's leading exports for a short time in the 1850s; in just 150 years, hundreds of thousands of hectares of ancient kauri forest disappeared, until protests in the 1940s halted the devastation. Reserves in Northland and Coromandel now safeguard the precious remaining stands of kauri forest. Waipoua State Forest south of Hokianga harbour shelters the largest trees, of which Tane Mahuta (51 m high, 14 m in diameter and 1200 years old) is the highest.

Northland and Auckland remain the most populous regions in New Zealand. 'A thousand suburbs in search of a city' is one description of Auckland, a sprawling metropolis that covers a massive 5300 km2 on either side of the Auckland isthmus. Its one million inhabitants, a quarter of New Zealand's population, live in nine cities incorporated into a single metropolitan area. The central city highrise of glass and steel houses the country's commercial centre and abuts New Zealand's principal port. Over 25 percent of Auckland's populace are either Maori or from Pacific Island cultures, making the city the world's largest Polynesian centre.

Balmy summers, beaches and sheltered waters make the north an ocean lover's eden. Nearby, Coromandel Peninsula and the Waitakere Range provide plenty of opportunities for trampers, but most Aucklanders and visitors choose to recreate on or by the sea: boating, fishing, diving or living life as an habitual beach dweller. Maritime parks protect coastal reserves and islands in the Hauraki Gulf and Bay of Islands. Amongst these, predator and browser free islands have assumed international significance as sanctuaries for endangered wildlife and plants lost from the mainland.

Left: Waitemata Harbour and Auckland's central city skyline.

Until recently Auckland was home to the America's Cup – the world's most prestigious yachting trophy. In a city mad about yachting, it's no surprise that one in ten Aucklanders owns a boat or yacht, many of which are located in Westhaven Marina (*far right*). The city is also New Zealand's most culturally diverse – the annual Pasifika Festival (*right*) brings the city's Pacific cultures to the fore. *Above*: The fountain at Mission Bay provides kids with a place to cool off.

Among the Far North's treasures are the expansive dunelands of Te Paki Farm Park (*far left*) at the top of 90 Mile Beach. The farm park is a scattered series of reserves providing habitat for native flora and fauna. A few kilometres on, Cape Reinga (*left*) is the place where Maori believe the spirits depart after death to be borne by ocean currents to their mythical home in Hawaiiki. *Above*: Bay of Islands.

Rangitoto Island in the Hauraki Gulf (*left*) last
erupted just 600 years ago. A protected reserve, a visit
to the island is a popular day excursion from Auckland. Pohutukawa blooms on Little Barrier Island
(*top*), one of the most important of New Zealand's
island sanctuaries for native species. *Above*: A rock
stack at sunset on Whatipu Beach at the entrance to
Auckland's Manukau Harbour.

Ocean swells surge against impressive cliffs north of Piha, on Auckland's west coast at the base of the Waitakere Range. Piha, just half an hour from central Auckland (*far right*), is both surfing mecca and holiday resort. The forest-covered Waitakere Range is a favourite haunt, a place to escape daily city life. The 1030 m Auckland Harbour Bridge (*right*) spans Waitemata Harbour, linking the central city with northern suburbs.

Rangitoto Island (*above*), a dormant volcano, lies on the eastern side of Rangitoto Channel off Auckland's North Shore, one of the city's wealthier suburbs. In the Bay of Islands, Kerikeri's Stone Store (*right*), built in 1835, is one of the oldest buildings in New Zealand. Historic sites and buildings in Kerikeri, Waitangi and Russell (*far right*, the former Russell police station) provide tangible links with this country's colonial past.

Tane Mahuta, the largest kauri in New Zealand, is
a short walk from SH 12 in Waipoua Forest, one of
the region's 'must visit' attractions. It took little more
than a century to decimate Northland's majestic kauri
forests – remnants now survive in reserves and forest parks throughout the region and in Coromandel.
Above: A kauri dam on Great Barrier Island.

Above: Remote dunelands at Parengarenga on the edge of Great Exhibition Bay, below North Cape.

Left: An old boatshed at Paihia, shuttered against the elements, on a balmy Bay of Islands evening. Messing about in boats is a prime activity in the Bay of Islands, which features numerous forested islands (*far left*), beaches and places of great historical importance. Marine mammal-watching, including dolphins and orca, is a popular tourist activity here.

Pohutukawa-lined beaches on the Coromandel Peninsula (*above*) between Thames and Coromandel. One of the North Island's best holiday destinations, Coromandel boasts fine beaches, a thriving arts community, and important Maori and colonial historic sites. Inland, the Coromandel Forest Park contains remnant kauri forest, is an important refuge for brown kiwi, and has some challenging tramping opportunities. The pick of Coromandel's beaches are at Whitianga, Whangamata and Waihi. *Right*: Coastline near Pauanui.

CENTRAL NORTH ISLAND

The Central North Island, a zone of active volcanism stretching from Mt Taranaki in the west to White Island off the Bay of Plenty coast, has been shattered by millennia of cataclysmic volcanic activity. These unimaginable forces have created a complex landscape of extinct, dormant and active volcanoes, and a spectacular region of geothermal activity – an impressive collective reminder of New Zealand's position on the Pacific Ring of Fire.

It is on the 'volcanic plateau', that encompasses Tongariro National Park and the Taupo-Rotorua geothermal areas, where the most vigorous indications of this spectacular activity are still encountered. Regular eruptions occur on Mts Ruapehu and Ngauruhoe, and on White Island. Volcanic ructions have dealt tragic consequences in recent times: the eruption of Mt Tarawera in 1886 and a tragic flood from Mt Ruapehu's crater lake in 1953 each claimed 150 lives. However, these are comparatively benign events when compared with past eruptions that spread volcanic debris far and wide over the North Island.

To Maori, who once heavily populated the volcanic plateau, Ruapehu, Ngauruhoe, Tongariro and Taranaki are sacred deities. In one often-told story, Taranaki was said to have fled to the west coast after a lost battle with Tongariro (carving the rent through which the Whanganui River now flows as he went). Ngati Tuwharetoa's reverence for the Tongariro volcanoes led to their summits being gifted to the nation as a national park in 1887. Tongariro National Park has since been granted dual World Heritage status in recognition of the cultural and natural significance of these volcanic landscapes.

Forestry, dairy farming and tourism are the predominant industries in this part of the country. Although soils deficient in some key minerals defeated many early volcanic plateau pastoralists, pine trees, in particular *Pinus radiata*, flourished in the impoverished conditions. This discovery led to widespread plantings north of Taupo in what became the world's largest afforestation scheme. Pastoralists enjoyed more success on the Waikato River's fertile plains, developing them into New Zealand's premier dairy farming area.

For more than a century, tourists have been journeying to the volcanic plateau to experience its natural wonders: Lake Taupo, the Tongariro volcanoes, Mt Tarawera, and Rotorua's geysers, fumaroles, mudpools, bubbling hot springs and silica formations. Large commercial skifields on Mt Ruapehu attract thousands each winter weekend, while adventure activities such as mountain-biking, kayaking and trout fishing have year-round adherents.

For several centuries the fastest route north to the volcanic plateau was up the Whanganui River – the country's longest navigable waterway. Rich in Maori folklore, history and scenery, the river begins as a trickle on the flanks of Mt Tongariro and thereafter weaves a 290 km path through forests and gorges that lie in the hinterland between the plateau and eastern Taranaki. Maori lived on its banks for 600 years, establishing both a spiritual and practical relationship with it. European missionaries and explorers were followed by paddle-steamers laden with tourists, modern day jetboats and recreationalists' canoes. Whanganui National Park, created in 1986, protects stands of lowland forest on the river's central and lower reaches.

Far from its mythical birthplace on the plateau, the elegantly shaped Mt Taranaki stands aloof on the west coast above its encircling ring plain. Taranaki's almost perfect symmetry is often compared with Japan's Mt Fuji. Like Fuji, and also Ngauruhoe and Tongariro, Taranaki is a classic andesitic volcano. Five years after it was sighted by Captain Cook in 1770, the mountain belched its last after 120,000 years of activity. Nonetheless, Taranaki is officially regarded as 'dormant', not extinct, and volcanologists don't rule out future activity. Egmont National Park's lower reaches, which encircle Taranaki, are dominated by forests of kamahi, rimu and rata, the remnants of a huge forest mostly converted to pasture after Europeans arrived in the 19th century. The new settlers discovered terrain made fertile by thousands of years of volcanic fallout; Taranaki's lush pastures have provided wealth for its numerous rural communities, principally from dairy farming. Discoveries of huge reservoirs of natural gas and smaller quantities of oil added a new economic focus – energy.

Left: Whirinaki Forest Park. *Overleaf*: The June 1996 eruption of Mt Ruapehu, in Tongariro National Park.

The beautiful limestone caves of the Waitomo area lie west of the Central North Island's volcanic heartland. Thousands of visitors a year enter this accessible cave system with its spectacular caverns, underground waterways, glowworm grottos and extraordinary formations of stalactites (*above*). At left, abseilers are seen making a daring descent into the vast Lost World Cave. On the surface, the Marokopa River tumbles over a limestone bluff en route to the west coast.

The Whanganui River is New Zealand's longest navigable river, used from the earliest days of human occupation as an access route from the coast to the Central North Island hinterland. Its upper reaches flow through Whanganui National Park. Canoeing down the river is the park's most popular recreational activity.

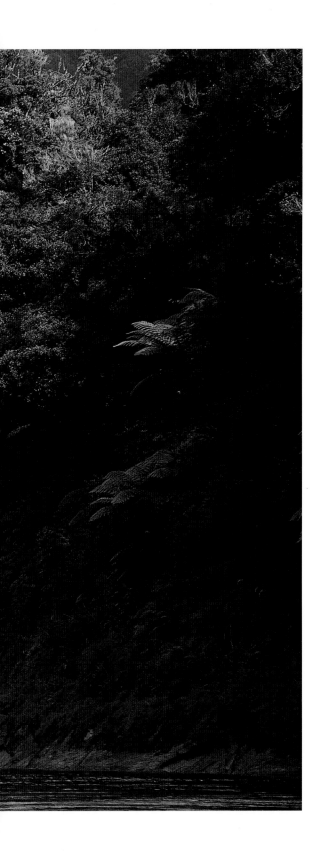

Whanganui National Park's virgin and regenerating forest contains populations of North Island brown kiwi (*top*), and other nationally endangered wildlife such as the blue duck and kaka. Ferns clinging to riverbanks (*above*) and below the forest canopy are commonly seen in the park.

Rotorua's geothermal wonders are world-renowned. Chief among these is Pohutu Geyser (*far left*) and the sparkling waters and mineral deposits in Waiotapu's Champagne Pool (*above*). The pool was formed 900 years ago by a hydrothermal explosion. *Left*: Volcanic White Island, lying off the Bay of Plenty coast, is another expression of the region's volcanic and geothermal activity. *Previous pages*: Snow-streaked Mt Ngauruhoe (foreground) and Mt Ruapehu, at sunrise.

These tranquil images of Lake Taupo belie the lake's devastating origins: a huge volcanic eruption – one of the largest ever in the world – thought to have occurred about 2000 years ago. The lake was stocked with trout in the 19th century and is now a renowned fly fishing destination. Lying between Tongariro National Park and the Rotorua geothermal region, Taupo is a major holiday centre.

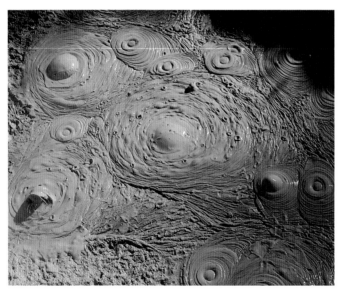

Blue Lake (*top*) on Mt Tongariro is one of several volcanic lakes seen on the popular 'Tongariro Crossing' tramping route. The mountains of Tongariro National Park are sacred to the Ngati Tuwharetoa tribe whose wharenui/meeting house (*right*) is located at Waihi on the shores of Lake Taupo. *Above*: Geothermal mudpools near Rotorua are thicker in summer when there is less rainwater. *Overleaf*: Arahaki Lagoon in Whirinaki Forest Park is flanked by 60 m high kahikatea forest, one of the last examples of these impressive forests remaining in the North Island.

Left and above: Mt Taranaki (2518 m), in Egmont National Park, is the most recent in a chain of volcanoes that have stood in the area north of the present peak over the past 2 million years. Mt Taranaki attracts climbers and trampers all year round. Bells Falls (*top*) is one of the highlights of the popular round the mountain tramp.

Three views of Central North Island rivers. *Left*: Just north of Taupo, the 425 km Waikato River is channelled through a narrow 15 m gut before it crashes spectacularly over the 11 m Huka Falls. Further downstream, the river backs up behind one of eight dams constructed between the 1920s and 1960s for hydro-electricity generation (*top*). The Whirinaki Gorge (*above*) is located in Whirinaki Forest Park.

EAST CAPE
HAWKE'S BAY

East Cape is a remote, mountainous domain given character by its spectacular coastline of bluffs and intimate beaches, its deeply corrugated hill country and a backdrop of forested ranges. At its heart is the Urewera wilderness in the Huiarau Range, a brooding, misted hinterland covered in dense forest and steeped in Maori folklore. Further north is the Raukumara Range whose seaward ridges fall toward the easternmost extremity of New Zealand's main islands, the East Cape.

Issuing from this angular landscape are a crush of rivers and streams that broaden as they near the coast to form the pockets of flat land which hold most East Cape settlements, including the major centre of Gisborne. Today the region is meagrely populated, its scattered rural communities linked by the tortuous roads that wind around the coast and through Te Urewera.

In few other parts of New Zealand have Maori cultural traditions survived as intact as they have done on the East Cape. Notwithstanding that Captain James Cook's first New Zealand landfall was at Poverty Bay in 1769, East Cape's rugged and inaccessible nature made it one of the last regions to be settled by the colonists who followed. Maori, who have at times fiercely resisted the new culture, today number more than 75 percent of East Cape's rural population and one third of Gisborne's urban population. Maori have resisted the drift to main centres, and have preferred to live close to their ancestral homelands, eking out a life from the land; traditional marae and meeting houses remain the centre of community life.

The Raukumara Range, and the Urewera district to the south, are enclaves of enormous spiritual importance to the Tuhoe and Ngati Porou tribes. Te Urewera National Park (214,000 ha), the largest expanse of native forest in the North Island, is forever associated with the Tuhoe 'children of the mist', while Ngati Porou hold allegiance to Mt Hikurangi (1752 m), the highest point in the Raukumara Range and the highest non-volcanic peak in the North Island. (It is often claimed that Mt Hikurangi is the first place on earth to receive the sun's rays each day.)

The legacy of deforestation on the exposed hill country lining the seaward flanks of these ranges tells another story – one of overwhelming land degradation. With each storm, denuded hillsides of soft, saturated mudstones slip into the valleys, turning rivers dirty brown and periodically triggering floods that inundate lowland communities and farms.

South of the Mahia Peninsula, Hawke's Bay presents a rather different visage with its broad plains, ordered fields, vineyards and large pastoral runs. Prosperity has come to this region from its produce – grains, fruits, vegetables and sheep – activities that were established by monied colonists who quickly saw potential in the land.

Napier and Hastings are the region's two main centres – two cities of about 55,000 and 59,000 respectively, situated within 30 minutes drive of each other. Devastated in 1931 by an earthquake that left 256 dead, revitalised seaside Napier has assumed the sobriquet of New Zealand's art deco capital, based on the flamboyant architectural style now prevalent in its streets. The wooded hinterland formed by the Kaweka and Ruahine ranges, a continuation of the North Island's mountainous spine, attracts more than 2000 mm of rain annually, in sharp contrast to the plain's reputation as one of the sunniest and driest areas in the country.

While Hawke's Bay, with its pleasant climate, beaches, wineries and architecture, may appear the more alluring of these two districts, East Cape offers rewards for the patient visitor. Remote villages and lonely pohutukawa-lined beaches along the 340 km coastal route between Opotiki and Gisborne exude a character lost from many other areas. The region has developed a reputation for its wine making and makes much of its historical associations with Captain Cook. The long journey to the Urewera wilderness and nearby Whirinaki forest is amply compensated by the experience of magnificent podocarp and beech forests – the protected remnants of an ancient natural order that has long since disappeared from the North Island lowlands.

Left: Wainui Beach, east of Gisborne.

Rolling hillcountry in the Tukituki valley (*left*), south of Havelock North, and in the Tiniroto Valley southwest of Gisborne (*top*) is prime sheep-farming country, the region's most important industry. The region's drier climate has also been a boon for farm forestry, winemaking and market gardening. *Overleaf*: Pohutukawa flowering at Wainui Beach, near Gisborne.

The region's coast is a spectacular combination of bluffs, headlands and beaches. The bluffs of Cape Kidnappers (*left*) jut into the Pacific at the southern end of Hawke Bay. Thousands of visitors go to the Cape each year to visit New Zealand's largest colony of Australasian gannets. Marau Point's wind and water-fluted headland south of Anaura Bay (*top*), is typical of the East Cape coast. In 1769, the British seafarer Captain James Cook stepped ashore in Poverty Bay (*above*), close to where the city of Gisborne now stands.

The blend of Maori and European culture in Hawke's Bay and the East Cape is often exemplified in its art and architecture: the National Tobacco Company building (*top*) is one of Napier's most famous art deco structures; the Ruatoria Memorial Hall (*above*) contains intricate Maori carvings and panels. *Left*: Poverty Bay. *Previous pages*: Korokoro Falls, Te Urewera National Park.

A tramper pauses at a viewpoint overlooking Lake Waikaremoana and Panekiri Bluff in Te Urewera National Park. The 214,000 ha park is the largest remaining unmodified forest in the North Island. Rugged and remote, the park is steeped in Maori history, and is a refuge for endangered species such as the kokako and brown kiwi. The 3–4 day walk around Lake Waikaremoana is one of the country's better-known tramps.

LOWER NORTH ISLAND

The forested Rimutaka and Tararua ranges are the southern-most expression of the North Island's mountainous spine that has its northern limit at East Cape. Pushed up by activity along an eastern-lying fault, the ranges divide east and western regions of the lower North Island, much as the Southern Alps segregate Westland from Canterbury. Set against this hilly backdrop are the fertile plains of Wairarapa on the east, and Manawatu, Horowhenua and the hill suburbs of greater Wellington on the west.

The characteristically rugged west coast rocky shores and cliffs southwest of Wellington eventually give way to long sandy surf beaches that arc northwards at the edge of the South Taranaki Bight. The coastal flood plains of Horowhenua and Manawatu have been turned into highly productive market gardens, and into mixed crop and dairy farms that generate sustenance for Wellington city and for export markets. The foothills rising gently against the Tararua Range have proved choice sheep farming country. Palmerston North, Manawatu's major urban centre, lies on the northern banks of the Manawatu River, just a few kilometres from the point where the river begins to force its way through a spectacular 16 km gorge between the Tararua and Ruahine ranges.

Wairarapa's landscape is a little more complex, occupying a series of broad plains, basins and hill country between the bluffed Pacific Coast and the ranges. Southern Wairarapa, where large pastoral runs were established by rich Wellington colonists, is the oldest farming region in New Zealand. A series of rural towns sprang up in their wake all the way to Hawke's Bay. Centres such as Dannevirke and Norsewood reflect their Danish and Norwegian founders – tireless workers responsible for clearing large areas of northern Wairarapa forest. The wild and inaccessible Wairarapa coastline runs 350 km between Cape Kidnappers and Cape Palliser, the North Island's southernmost point, The surf beaches at Castlepoint and Riversdale are two locations where one can marvel at the stark natural beauty of this coastline.

Wellington, the nation's capital, has a cosmopolitan population of around 160,000, including concentrations of Pacific, Asian and European ethnic communities. When combined with neighbouring Porirua and the Hutt Valley, greater Wellington is New Zealand's second largest urban area with around 400,000 people. It is the country's political and financial centre – the home of Parliament, accompanying government departments, lobbyists and major companies. While some would argue that all of New Zealand is at risk from earthquakes, that risk is acutely felt in Wellington, which, unbeknown to its European founders, was built across a major fault line. The threat of a major earthquake has contributed to the transformation of downtown Wellington, which was once redolent with splendid Victorian architecture. Steel and glass now rise against hill suburbs where old villas retain something of the city's original character. The last big earthquake in 1855 raised the seabed two metres, creating much of the flat land central Wellington is now located on, and the shelf that carries the Hutt motorway.

Although the city is bedevilled by its reputation as one of the windiest cities in the world, Wellingtonians are able to seek solace from the elements in any one of its cafes, galleries, bars and ethnic eateries. The city's reputation as a centre for music and the arts has grown in recent years as the biennial international arts festival and the City Art Gallery attests. However it is Te Papa – New Zealand's national museum – which stands out as the city's premier attraction.

The destruction of wilderness has been no less felt in the lower North Island, but the success of restoration efforts at Wellington's Karori Wildlife Sanctuary, the Kapiti Island Nature Reserve and Wairarapa's Mt Bruce Wildlife Centre are showing the way ahead. These places offer renewed hope for endangered species such as brown kiwi, kaka and saddleback. Each of these places is open to the public, offering an opportunity to experience a small reminder of primeval New Zealand.

Left: Castlepoint, on the Wairarapa coast. *Overleaf*: Dawn, Oriental Bay, Wellington

Te Papa Tongarewa, or 'Te Papa' is New Zealand's national museum. Opened in 1998, it quickly became a domestic and international tourist drawcard. Te Papa houses important national collections of Maori, Pacific and European art and culture and tells the stories of New Zealand's unique flora and fauna and the dynamic forces that shaped the land, and of its discovery by Pacific voyagers and later European colonisers.

Parliament House (*top*) in Central Wellington is the hub of political life in New Zealand. Built in 1922, the building has recently been refurbished and earthquake strengthened. The Cable Car (which links Wellington City with Victoria University and the Botanic Gardens) is another icon in a city also renowned for its nightlife and cafés.

Kapiti Island, north of Wellington, is one of New Zealand's most important wildlife preserves. After a major effort to rid the island of predators, the island is now a refuge for many critically endangered species. Wellington, known as the 'windy city', is battered regularly by the predominant northerly, making for exciting boating conditions in Wellington Harbour (*left*), and testing conditions for aircraft pilots! (*far left*). *Overleaf:* Martinborough's vineyards produce some of the nation's finest wines. (Photograph: Kevin Judd)

First published in 2003 by Craig Potton Publishing
98 Vickerman Street, PO Box 555, Nelson, New Zealand
www.craigpotton.co.nz

© 2003 Craig Potton Publishing
Photography © Craig Potton © Individual photographers
Reprinted in 2004,2005

ISBN 1 877333 05 0

Filmwork by Image Centre, Auckland, New Zealand
Printed in China by Everbest Printing Co. Ltd